I CAN
READ ABOUT

CAVES

Written by C. J. Naden

Illustrated by Virginia McWilliams

Troll Associates

Many years ago, a cowboy and his horse almost fell into a big hole in the ground. The cowboy could not believe his eyes. The hole seemed to go on forever! The cowboy had discovered the Carlsbad Caverns in New Mexico, one of the biggest cave systems in the world.

A cave is a natural hole in the earth. It is big enough for a person to enter. Most caves are dark and gloomy. Water drips from the ceiling. The air is moist. Bats and rats and snakes and salamanders wander about in the dark.

But some caves, like Carlsbad, are truly beautiful.
Carlsbad is a limestone cave. Most caves are hollowed out
of soft rock such as limestone. These caves are sometimes
called *caverns*.

Some of the big caverns were made millions of years ago.

This is how a cave or cavern is born.
Water seeps through the earth, making cracks in soft rock.
After a long time, the water wears paths through the rock.
The paths widen into tunnels. After many, many years the
tunnels widen into huge rooms. Water fills the rooms and
tunnels and paths. The water keeps eating away at the rock.

Then pressure from inside the earth causes the soft rock to break or tilt. The water seeps out of the cave. As the water drains away, air enters the cave. But some water still drips into the cave through cracks in the rock. But now, the water changes the cave into a strange, underground world of beauty.

What is a *stalactite?*

A single drop of water forms on the cave ceiling. When the water dries up, a tiny speck of lime remains. Another drop forms, and another, all in the same place. Each time the water dries up, a little more lime crystal is left. The crystals grow into a stone "icicle."

The icicle is called a stalactite.

Sometimes the drops of water fall onto the cave floor. They build pointed stone icicles from the ground up. These are called *stalagmites*. Here is one way to remember which is which: stalactite has "c" for *ceiling*; stalagmite has a "g" for *ground*.

Some stalactites and stalagmites become very big and thick. They grow at different rates. Some may take one hundred years to grow one inch, or 2.5 centimeters. Others grow that much in a year. How fast they grow depends on how much water seeps into the cave and how much lime the water contains.

Sometimes a stalactite and stalagmite grow so large that they meet each other. Then they form a limestone *column*.

Water builds other strange cave shapes.
Sometimes water oozes from the ceiling and forms
a "curtain" of stone down one wall. This is called
a *calcite curtain* or *dripstone curtain*.

Sometimes the water forms
delicate-looking stone flowers
or tiny "pearls." Some twirly, twisting
stalactites grow up, down, and sideways.
No one knows why.

There are other kinds of caves besides caverns.
Sea caves are made by waves pounding against
rocky cliffs. The waves wear away the rocks, scooping out a cave.

One of the world's best-known sea caves is the Blue Grotto.
It is on the island of Capri in Italy. "Grotto" means cave.
The Blue Grotto gets its name from the blue color of the water.

The largest sea cave in North America is in Oregon. It is called
the Sea Lion Cave because sea lions raise their families there.

Ice caves have walls and roofs of
ice. Some ice caves have been hollowed
out of glaciers. Inside the cave in
Paradise Glacier in Washington,
the ice has formed strange bumps
and wrinkles all over the ceiling
and walls of the cave.

There are lava caves in Hawaii and some western states. These caves form when hot melted rock, called *lava,* flows from the ground. The lava may leave behind a hollow tube or bubble. When the lava cools and hardens, a cave is formed. Lava caves are not usually very deep under the ground.

Bones and stone tools and bits of charcoal have been found inside caves. Scientists say that the stone tools discovered in the caves of southern France may be 500,000 years old. They were left there by early cave dwellers—some of the first people on earth. Most caves, however, do not make very good homes. They are too wet and too dark and too cold for people to live in.

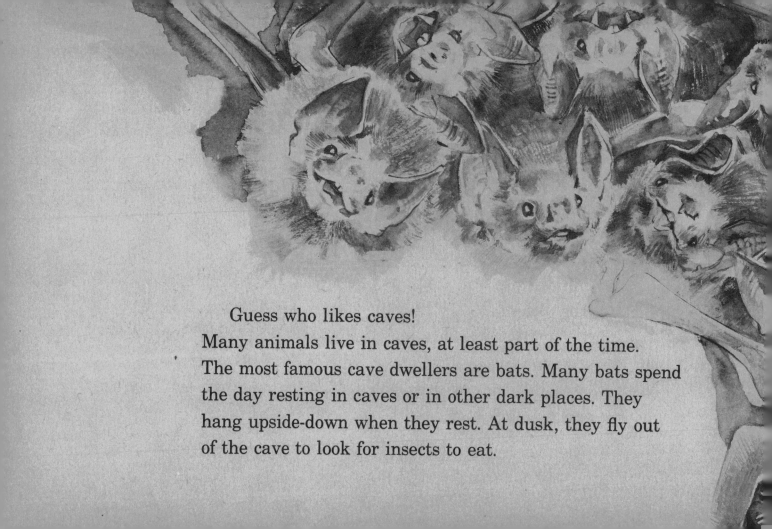

Guess who likes caves!
Many animals live in caves, at least part of the time.
The most famous cave dwellers are bats. Many bats spend
the day resting in caves or in other dark places. They
hang upside-down when they rest. At dusk, they fly out
of the cave to look for insects to eat.

Bats usually live in groups. Sometimes thousands of bats cover the walls and ceilings of a cave.

Some bears live in caves during the winter. When the weather gets cold, the bear looks around for a warm, snug cave or some other kind of den. Then it settles down to wait for spring. Sometimes, on a mild winter day, the bear wakes up and walks around. Sometimes it just wakes up and grumbles. A bear eats very little during the winter. It lives off its own stored body fat.

Winter is also the time when baby bears are born.

In the spring, when bears leave
the den, they are very hungry.

There are other animals that spend part of their time near or around caves. Snakes curl up for winter. Some skunks raise their young in caves. Many insects sleep through the cold weather in the shelter of caves. And birds often build their nests near the entrance to a cave.

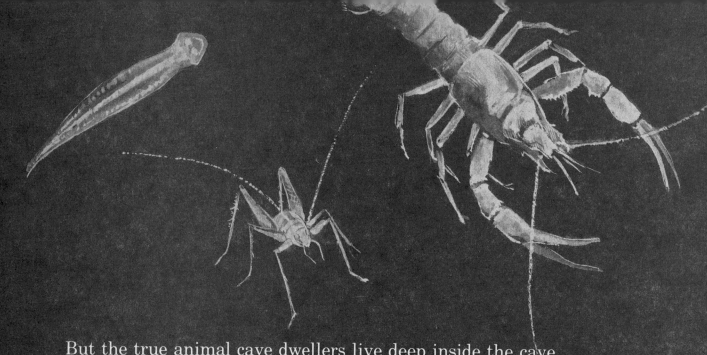

But the true animal cave dwellers live deep inside the cave
in constant darkness. Among them are certain kinds of fish, insects,
shrimp, and salamanders. Generations of these animals have spent their
entire lives in caves. Some have lost their coloring and are transparent.
Others are very pale or white.

Some are blind. But they do not need to see. Instead, they
have a good sense of smell, or touch, or hearing. Blindfish can
sense even the slightest movement in the water. Cave crickets find
their food with their long feelers.

Tiny blind salamanders
are very rare. Some cave salamanders
are able to see at birth. But later,
their eyelids grow together.

Although some animals can live
in total darkness, most plants cannot.
Green plants need light to grow.
But mushrooms and molds will grow in
the moist darkness of caves.

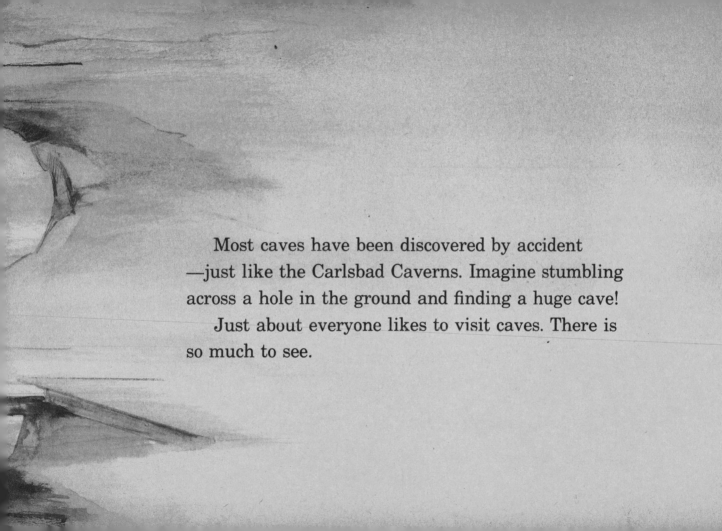

Most caves have been discovered by accident
—just like the Carlsbad Caverns. Imagine stumbling
across a hole in the ground and finding a huge cave!

Just about everyone likes to visit caves. There is
so much to see.

In the Carlsbad Caverns, there is a room called the "Big Room." It is so huge that ten football fields could fit inside. At one point, the ceiling is as high as a thirty-story building. It is covered with limestone icicles. Some of the passages in Carlsbad go more than one thousand feet, or 300 meters, under the ground.

Some of the deepest caves in the world are in France.
Some go down more than three thousand feet, or 910 meters.
Prehistoric paintings cover the walls of some caves in
France and Spain.

Their colors are still bright after 15,000 years.

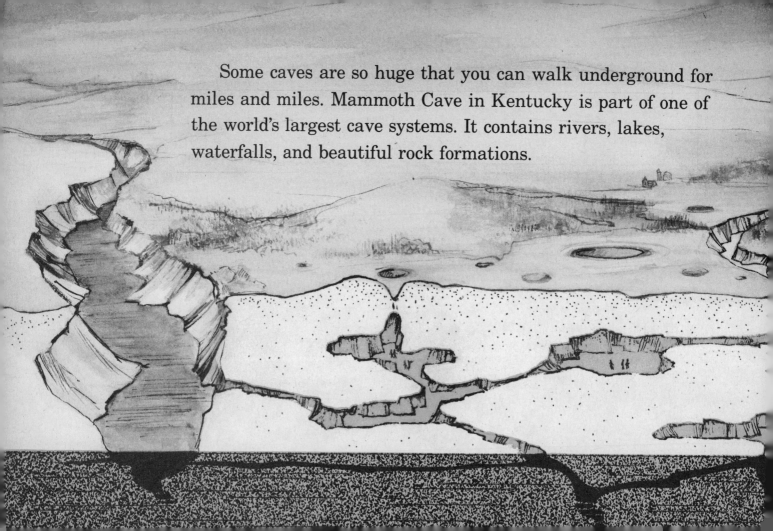

Some caves are so huge that you can walk underground for miles and miles. Mammoth Cave in Kentucky is part of one of the world's largest cave systems. It contains rivers, lakes, waterfalls, and beautiful rock formations.

In Iceland, visitors can go to a deep lava cave to hear their own echoes. In New Zealand, they can watch the greenish-blue light of thousands and thousands of glowworms on the cave walls. And in Austria, they can visit beautiful caves filled with underground glaciers and strange ice formations.

Many of the world's caves have not yet been fully explored. But there always seems to be someone who is willing to brave the unknown. People who explore caves are called *spelunkers*.

Spelunking, or cave exploring, can be fun. But it can be dangerous, too. Sometimes cave explorers must squeeze through narrow passages or cross icy, underground streams. They often wear waterproof suits to keep dry. Sometimes they must climb down rope ladders to get to a lower level in a cave.

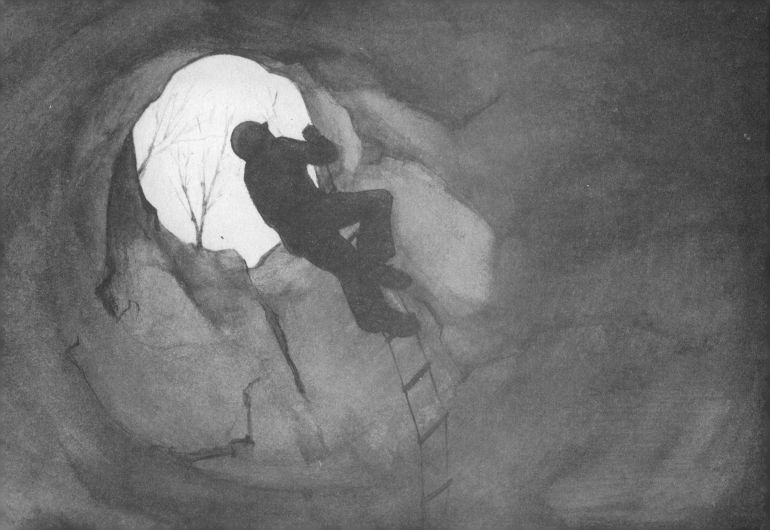

For most people, a guided tour is exciting enough. Sometimes, when you are deep inside a cave, your tour guide will turn off the lights.

Everything is dark and still and cool.
Suddenly, you hear a fluttering sound.
Is it a bat?

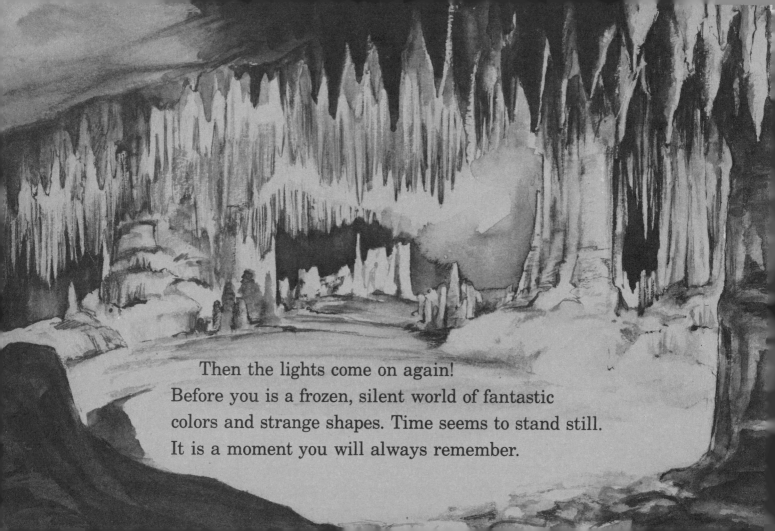

Then the lights come on again!
Before you is a frozen, silent world of fantastic
colors and strange shapes. Time seems to stand still.
It is a moment you will always remember.